Modern Living

Modern Living

edited by Franco Magnani

Studio Vista London

© Görlich Editore S.p.A., Milan 1972
Original edition published in Italy under the title
Vivere Moderno
Edited by Görlich Editore, Milan
Translated into English by Pearl Sanders
Published in Great Britain in 1973 by Studio Vista
35 Red Lion Square, London WC1
Filmset in Great Britain by Ramsay Typesetting, London and Crawley
Printed in Italy
ISBN 0 289 70378 6

The entrance hall

Entrance hall – the visitor receives his first impression here. Today the entrance hall, though sometimes very small, fulfils a modest but precise function. It serves as a passageway, a lobby for coats and umbrellas, a place to chat on the 'phone. Even when it opens on to the living-room, it can impose its own tone on the whole décor, and merits no less attention than do the more 'important' living areas.

1
Entrance hall leading into the living-room: architects
Pino Pini and Ettore Zerbi. The lowered ceiling and
raised floor create a dynamic and attractive architectural
effect; the touches of colour are carefully placed.
Felt-covered walls.

2
Small entrance hall of a flat in Udine: architect Ennio
Ghiggio. Interesting features are the telephone bracket
in white enamelled wood, and the textural effects in the
door's white fabric cover, emphasized by the dark
surround.

2

3
Hall decorated in neutral and cold tones. Standard coat
hangers. Furnished by Franco Menna.

3

4
Combined hall and cloakroom in a small flat.
Architects Pino Pini and Ettore Zerbi. A section of the
ceiling has been lowered to break the uniformity of an
over-long corridor. Standard coat hanger in black
enamelled beech.

4

5
Tiny hall, only separated from the living-room by a
pillar. Bookshelves by Lips-Vago.

5

6
Entrance hall communicating directly with the main
living-room in a flat furnished by architects L. Ferrari
and P. Martano. A low storage unit accentuates the
length of the room and indicates the various activities
which take place in it.

The staircase

Staircase – no longer purely functional, but a feature of aesthetic importance, and sometimes the main focus of volume and colour values. A careful choice of materials should be made and particular emphasis placed on structure: in some staircases the steps are raised, emerging from axial beams. Ideally, one should combine aesthetic considerations with the functional.

1
Living-room furnished by Piero Sadun. The wooden
gloss-painted staircase is a central feature of the décor.

2
Remodelled staircase in an old building: architect L. Gallarini. The walls are covered in straw with decorations in orange canotex. The steps and sides of the staircase are entirely covered in carpet, the handrails are walnut.

2

3
Staircase in a modernized house. Covered throughout in the same carpet as is used in the flat. Furnished by Piero Pinto.

3

4
An elegant staircase of wood and metal which blends perfectly with the décor. Furnished by architect G. L. Volpi. Walnut treads with lowered edge to enable the green carpet to be fitted. Handrail padded and covered in tufted fabric.

5
In this home in an attic interest is focused on the staircase; it leads to a small loft which has been cleverly accentuated and incorporated into the design by means of a lively pattern of white stripes. Furnished by architects Claudia and Giuseppe Turchini.

5

6
Striking chrome staircase in the studio-home of a
young Paris photographer. One might have to be an
acrobat to use it, but its clear line blends perfectly with
its surroundings and with the ultra-modern furnishings.

The living-room

Living-room – a room in which to relax and feel at home, to talk, look and listen, to cut ourselves off from the outside world and surround ourselves with the objects we love best. It is a room which must serve us, not others. It should therefore not be planned with a view to creating an impression, but should be as personal as we can make it, even where we have to make use of mass-produced furniture.

1

Large living-room in an attic; furnished by architect E. Peduzzi Riva. The dining area is at the rear and separated from the living-room by a storage unit made of wood and laminated plastic. The lounge area is shown in the foreground. Note the long enamel-coated wooden shelf above the windows, which counters the steep incline of the far wall.

2
Dining table designed by Fabrizio Cocchia. A plastic
square table, with flaps opening outwards and upwards
in the form of a petal. Produced by Sormani.

3
Living-room in a flat furnished by Pino Pini and Ettore Zerbi. Interest is focused on the louvre blind which covers the entire surface of a wall; when this is closed, it completely shuts off the outside world.

4
Living-room in an attic with one floor-section raised.
Designed by Colombi and Guzzetti.

4

5
The lounge area of a huge living-room aimed at
prestige. The bar counter is made of concrete varnished
with a brilliant vinyl polish. The dining table is seen in
the foreground.

6
Small comfortable living-room produced from an
existing trapezoid-shaped room. Architects D. and C.
Aroldi. Moquette flooring, ceiling lined with walnut
beams, walls covered in felt.

6

7
Section of a rather theatrical French living-room,
characterized by the use of 'natural' materials. Cork (on
the walls), wood and fur create an unusual décor.

8

8
A 'youthful' living-room, sparsely furnished with
inflatable chairs and gloss-painted wooden cubes,
which can be arranged as desired at a moment's notice.
A lively effect is created by the colour.

9

9
Detail of the living-room in a photographer's studio
home (another part of the same house is illustrated on
page 20). The large lamp in the foreground (by Ingo
Maurer) lights the living and dining areas
simultaneously.

10

10-11
Large combined living and dining room for a house in
Germany. Architects Klaus and Gudrun Vogel. The
dining area is raised and separated from the rest of the
room by a large storage unit (lined on the reverse with
bookshelves). Wooden benches run along the window
and wall areas.

11

12

12
The entrance hall and living-room are combined in this little flat furnished by architects De Bevilacqua and Viganò. The pale carpet and the blue fabric covering the walls create a harmonious colour scheme, in which the only glaring note is the red of the accessories and sliding doors.

13
Large living-room in a home modernized by Franco Menna. The music equipment (specially designed furniture with built-in speakers) and the book units are painted in the same shade of violet-blue. The daring juxtaposition of the chestnut-coloured settee is attenuated by the neutral tones used for the other settee and the cushions.

14
Bed-sitter in a bachelor flat in Rome. On three levels.
The large divan is patterned in black and white leather
squares and gives this little room its distinctive
character. Bookshelves of perspex, steel and glass.

14

15
Large combined living and dining room in an old
house, modernized and furnished in clean lines and
quiet tones; the large Doraz painting introduces the one
violent colour note. The dining table is seen in the
foreground. The central part of the door has been
replaced with glass to provide a greater sense of
continuity. Lamps by Flos.

16
Lounge corner in a small living-room furnished with
settees designed by A. Rascaroli and pieces in the
Driade series, both produced by Astori Arredamenti.

The study

Study – the place where we read, write or pursue our hobbies. It may be quite separate or an integral part of the home. We may have simple work-benches supported by two trestles, bookshelves, bright engravings decorating the walls: each of us can furnish the study in his own way, both to make it functional and to satisfy our personal taste. However, in cases where professional considerations are involved the study must be such that a relationship of esteem and trust can be established with a possible client, and a greater degree of comfort may then be called for.

1
In this study-corner the austere furnishings are
brightened by early-twentieth-century posters on one
of the walls. This is a new idea for wall decoration.

2

A doctor's private study. The walls are completely covered in walnut panelling and furnished with work-benches and shelves to hold books and journals; chair designed by Breuer and produced by Gavina. Furnished by architects De Bevilacqua and Viganò.

2

3

A collector's private study; architect G. Veneziani. Thonet chair, nineteenth-century desk; the Art Nouveau cornerpiece has been extended by two benches running along the walls. The lamps are modern, as indeed is the concept underlying the whole, quite distinctive, décor.

4
A young person's study; the furniture consists of plain tables and chairs, but considerable importance is given to books, photos and personal objects arranged in a somewhat casual manner. Furnished by L. Ricciarini.

5
A plain table and four bookshelves fixed to the wall guarantee the minimum of privacy required for reading and study in the small space available.

6
Working area for three students, furnished with plain tables, a few chairs, bookshelves, and a generous use of colour. The furniture can easily be rearranged.

6

7
A brilliant method of redesigning a professional office.
The sparse furnishings and the clearcut juxtaposition of
three colours – grey, red and white – create a bright
décor which is further animated by the pattern of
reflections created by the aluminium wall covering.

8
A studio generating a calm working atmosphere; the adjustable bookshelves, small armchairs and trestle table are painted yellow, producing a lively décor rather than the bare functionalism so often evident even in places designed for creative work. Architect Colombi.

9
Studio designed by the Riva Studio for a sculptress. All
the furniture is on castors.

The fireplace

Fireplaces – in the modern home the fireplace no longer has only a practical function; it often appears in a decorative and symbolic capacity. In order to restore the traditional significance of the hearth it must justify its presence on a formal level. Even today in the case of country and weekend homes, the fireplace may still represent a quite efficient source of heat, and is then most successfully employed.

1
Fireside corner consisting of a small, but comfortable, space simply utilized to contain a settee and shelves for favourite books.

2
Small fireside in an attic, furnished by architects
Claudia and Giuseppe Turchini. The base and·upper
sections are lined in tiles. The furniture consists of
pouffs, an inflatable chair and bookshelves.

3
The fireplace is the outstanding feature of this living-
room furnished by architect M. Foltran. It introduces a
dynamic element into the rear wall, so that the entire
left corner is a pattern of overlapping planes,
accentuated by the fir-wood beams.

4

5

4 A small fireplace with chimney-cowl of an unusual shape, designed for a country house. Architect Einecke.

5 A small traditional-style fireplace, with plastered chimney-cowl, for a country house. Architect Hans Auras.

6 With little money but plenty of imagination two young

6

artists have furnished their simple home in an attic. The fireplace was there already, but it has now become the focal point of heat and colour for the entire room. This is an example of how a fireplace can create diversity in a large wall area or even become the pivot of a whole room. This is true not only for country houses, but for city homes as well.

Fireside area for conversation and reading in a
mountain village house furnished by architects Antonia

and Enrico Astori. The brickwork base of the stove is
continued and reaches the low stands along the walls.
Plated chimney-cowl with conical fitting.

The lounge

Lounge – a settee, a couple of armchairs, a coffee table, one or two storage units, are all that is needed to make a lounge. The important thing is to create an atmosphere of comfort and relaxation; lighting and colour are important factors in this. Standard, wall or table lamps are particularly useful, and in rooms which contain a fireplace, the lounge will probably be the fireside area.

1
Lounge designed by Piero Pinto, furnished in Square settees designed by Zanuso for Arflex, small chrome glass-topped table designed by Pinto. On the walls a modern drawing and small nineteenth-century pictures

appear side by side. In the foreground is a deep rocking chair made of polyurethane foam of graduated thickness and without a rigid structure, designed by Cini Boeri.

2
Lounge area in a bed-sitting room. The round bed
folds away into a settee. Designed by Ferradini and
Ferrari.

2

3
In this lounge furnished by Sergio Mazza and Giuliana
Gramigna the Full settees designed by the same
architects are placed at an angle to a service table in
the corner. The lounge and dining areas are combined
in this room, as we see from the set table in the
foreground.

4

4
Lounge area of a room built on two levels. The simple furnishings complete an area whose architecture alone is rich in providing design possibilities. Architect Nelly Kraus.

5
The black lacquered cocktail cabinet partitions the small lounge from the dining area in a design by Sergio

5

Mazza and Giuliana Gramigna. Full settee, Frau armchair, chrome steel table.

6 *Overpage*
Seen from the attic, a lounge built around the hearth in a country house furnished by Studio Tetrarch. Coronado settees designed by Tobia Scarpa. Note the fine terracotta tiled flooring.

Music

Music – constantly developing techniques provide us with superb reproduction equipment to give us music which is perfect in tone and readily available. It is not difficult to integrate this equipment into the overall furnishing of a home. The most important consideration in the case of hi-fi equipment is the siting of the sound boxes: each case must be treated individually.

1
Music corner with television and amplifier.

2
Automatic record changer and amplifier.

3
Stereo equipment incorporated in a centrally placed
unit designed by Claudio Salocchi for Sormani.
Furnishing by the same architect. The same unit serves
also as a small bookcase.

3

4

Living-room furnished by architects Pini and Zerbi. The pillar is encircled by a wooden bench on which are placed record player and stereo hi-fi amplifier. The speakers belonging to the system are arranged in a low bookcase at the other side of the room.

4

5

Unit for music equipment in a living-room dominated by a pillar. Designed by Colombi and Guzzetti.

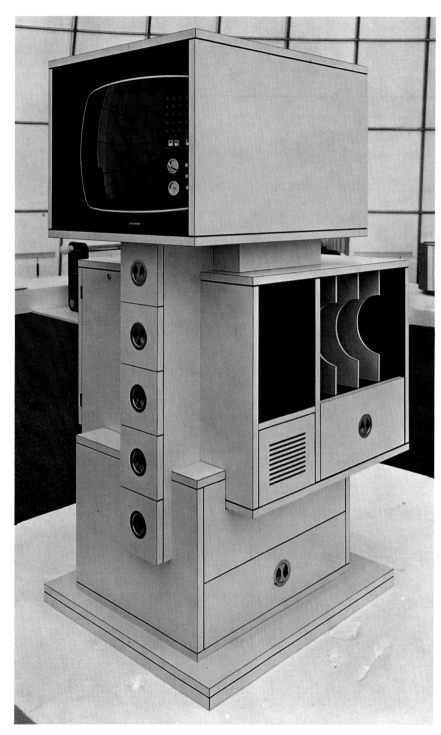

6
Centre unit consisting of several dovetailing volumes to accommodate TV, radio and records. Designed by Faleschini for Maspero.

Bookshelves

Bookshelves – the most usual methods of displaying books are on shelves, with or without glass, or on benches, but each of us can find his own solution to the problem. Books will often represent the most colourful, frequently-changing and exciting element in a décor – and this is no less true of cheap paperbacks than of first editions. Even where space is limited, any niche or corner or an empty space by a pillar may be transformed into a small library, a world of our own, with the aid of simple shelving.

1
Study area with bookshelves in enamelled wood for an American villa. Architects Gwatmey, Henderson and Siegel. The simple basic furnishings emphasize the architectural features of the house.

2
Study corner. The library is simply wall shelving coated
in laminated plastic. Nineteenth-century table and
chair. Furnished by Piero Pinto.

3
Study corner. White enamelled metal bookshelving
by Lips Vago. Simple trestle table and small chairs, also
of metal. The décor is rational and clean-cut, but not
without warmth. The Trevira window blind provides a
diffused light for reading.

4
A very suitable material for a rational and contemporary library is shelving in Cycolac, a Marbon ABS resin; they are designed by Marcello Siard and produced by Kartell. They have a uniform depth of 30 cm. (12 ins.), and are made in three lengths: 45, 65 and 80 cm. (18, 25 and 31 ins.), and four colours: white, orange, red and black.

4

5
Library with metal shelving for books and objects. The big plastic armchair is produced by Zanotta and designed by D'Urbino, De Pas and Lomazzi.

5

6
Enamel-coated wooden shelving for books and objects,
creating a corner for recreation in the large living-room.
Furnished by Annamaria and Alberto Carrain.

6

7
In this collector's room furnished by architect G.
Veneziana, the large library is contained in wooden
shelving placed in the under-roof area.

8
In a small flat furnished with good taste and simplicity
by architect Gianfranco Pagliettini, one of the two Lips
Vago bookcases acts as a partition to divide off the
dining area, without isolating it.

The kitchen

Kitchen – always particularly receptive to contemporary trends; the kitchen is lived in to a far greater extent than was formerly the case, since the traditional domestic staff have gradually been disappearing from the scene. It is nearly always here that breakfast is taken, and often lunch also. The kitchen is therefore a more 'habitable' room than it used to be, and colour has assumed an increasing importance as a means of making the room pleasant, without depriving it of its traditional functional characteristics.

1
Kitchen which includes the dining area, for a person living alone. Furnished by Franco Menna. The imitation bamboo iron table is lacquered black and glass-topped.

Kitchen designed by Vico Magistretti for Schiffini; the
material used is wood protected by polyurethane
varnish.

3
Kitchen with plexiglass containers. The revolving table
makes breakfasting easier. Designed by Marzio Cecchi.

4
Colour is an important element in this cheerful kitchen designed by Brusadelli for Lamber.

5
A kitchen produced by a German company, Osta. The tray tops to some of the drawer cupboards are fitted to hold small electric gadgets.

6
The kitchen of the future? A prototype exhibited at the Cologne Fair, designed for Bulthaup by a group of designers working in Ulm. Certainly, it is highly functional, but perhaps it savours of a space-ship.

5

6

7 Kitchen for a small flat with sober and rational
furniture designed by architect Roberto Barbieri.
Enamelled wooden cupboards designed by Tito Agnoli,
table and chairs by Aalto (distributed in Italy by Finn
Form). Lamp designed by Castiglioni for Flos.

8 Kitchen with a central block, communicating directly
with the living-room, designed for a Venetian villa and
furnished by architect G. Vedova. This example presents
greater scope and breadth of vision than the preceding
examples. Cherrywood furniture with white-enamelled
sections.

8

9
Tiny kitchen in a French designer's elegant flat. A
simple wall section fitted out as a bar divides the
working area from the rest of the living room.

The dining room

Dining room – or rather, the dining area, which in present-day homes has taken the place of the dining room. The furnishing is fairly standardized: a table, four or six chairs, a unit to contain the tableware. Sometimes a carpet or partitions define the dining area more clearly and separate it, if only visually, from the remainder of the home. For the furniture new styles and materials are sought, and to the wood of tradition are now added glass, plastic and metal.

1
Dining area in a flat furnished by Piero Pinto. An original feature is the juxtaposition of the plain straw-bottomed chairs and the glass-topped table with metal supports. Arco lamp designed by Castiglioni.

2
Dining area in an American designer's flat. The table
and plain Vienna straw chairs create a simple and
attractive 'corner', together with the ironical and
unexpected presence of the flag-panel. Furnishings by
Jim Howell.

2

3
Dining corner with Loto table and Locus-solus chairs
by Gae Aulenti, distributed by the Design Centre. The
lamp is by Stilnovo. Furnished by architect A. Baletti.

3

4
Dining area picked out by being slightly raised from the rest of the living-room. Designed by Carlo Bartoli.

4

5
A simple but well-furnished corner for the home of two young artists. Seats by Bassi, icosahedric lamp designed by Claude; on the low table, a lamp by Jacobsen.

5

6

6
Dining corner in a décor by Marcello Pietrantoni,
architect. The table is an old family piece; the leather
settee is designed by Van der Rohe for Knoll.

7

7
Dining area communicating with the living-room in a
German villa. Architects Witzemann and Stadelmaier.

8
This dining corner is concealed in the daytime and emerges from its cupboard when required, complete with chairs and food trolley. This is a new and interesting solution to the problem of finding enough space in a small flat, and can be achieved by the use of Pellicano shelving fitted for dining use. Design by V. Introini for Saporiti.

8

9
Dining corner for a Swiss villa. Furnished by architects Bartoli and Kummer. 'Meeting' table designed by Bartoli and Menichetti for Arflex; Mito seats in the T.70 range.

9

10
Dining corner in a décor by Maspes Romegalli, architect. The chairs are by the now classical Thonet, and the table is by Cassina. The severity of the dark colours is mitigated by the brightly contrasting painting and green lampshade.

10

11
In a small flatlet furnished by architect G. Ausenda, the corner serving the double function of dining area and study is furnished with Damaso adjustable shelving designed by the same architect for Ny Form. Thonet chairs enamelled white, like the table. Lighting by means of small ceiling spotlights.

11

12

In this interior designed by architect A. Astori, the dining area is simply separated from the rest of the living-room.

13

The original Topogo table with rounded edges.

14

Dining area in a flat built on two levels, furnished by architect G. L. Volpi.

12

14

13

15
Dining area with Boffi units which screen off the
sleeping accommodation.

The bedroom

Bedroom – the most private and personal room in the whole flat; often accompanied by a dressing room, it becomes a room which is complete in itself. The furniture is basic: a bed, small bedside tables, a wardrobe, sometimes a dressing table or chests of drawers. Where space permits, the bed may be placed in the centre of the room, and it is with this arrangement in mind that circular beds have now been designed. The colours chosen are usually restful.

1
Bedroom furnished by architect A. Mosca. The leather-covered bed has a chrome base, as do the units on either side of it. Designed by the same architect for Cinova. The functional lighting is by Flos.

2
Bedroom furnished by architect Ennio Ghiggio. The
bed is by Arcibed and is made of expanded
polyurethane, covered in blue woven fabric. Paintings
by Guidi and Cantatore. Below the window is a shelf
containing drawers and inserted beauty case, in pale
blue lacquer. The chests of drawers on either side of
the bed may also be used as seats.

2

3
Small adjustable Chica armchair of polystyrole, for the
children's room. Designed by Decursu, De Pas,
D'Urbino.

4

5

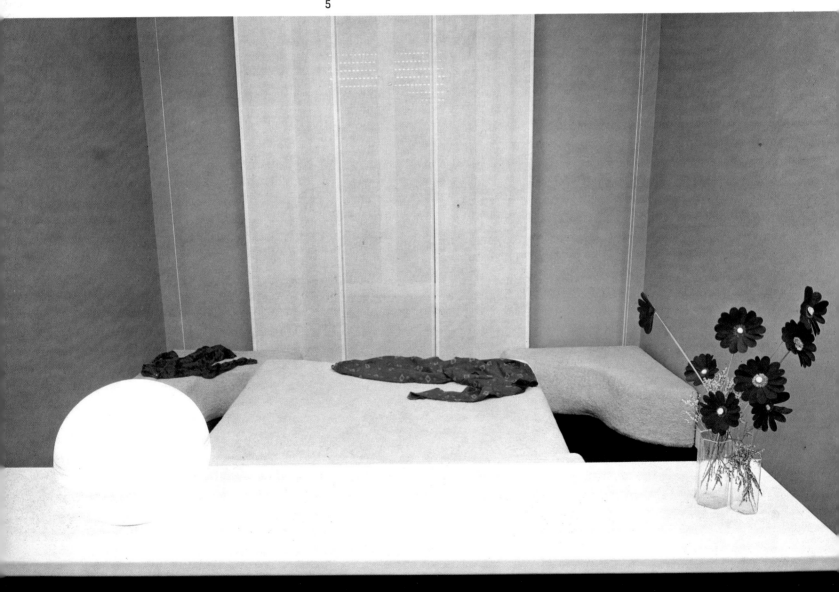

4
Divan for a young person's room designed by Astori.
Driade units.

5
Simple elegance is the keynote of this bedroom
furnished by Franco Menna. The headboard consists of
a storage unit, the bedside tables are cubes.

6
A bedroom reduced to essentials: the bed stands in
the centre on a base which serves as a storage unit and
is covered in carpet, like the rest of the flooring.

7
View of a bedroom furnished by Gianfranco Pagliettini, architect. The bed is by I. C. F. De Padova; a lacquered wooden cube acts as a bedside table; round cushion-seats.

7

8
A simple bedroom. The flower motif on the bed-cover is repeated on the curtain. Designed by Studio Punto Tre.

9
Bed with fur cover designed by architect Claudio Salocchi for Sormani.

8

9

10
A young man's bedroom furnished with adjustable units
produced by Studio Dierre.

10

11
A simple bedroom, enlivened by a few touches of
colour in an interior designed by architects Alberto
Colombi and Paolo Guzzetti. The dressing area is
divided from the bedroom by a white plastic screen and
slightly raised.

12
This very bright bedroom relies for its effect on the
interplay of the colours of the bed cover, cushions and
paintings. The ivory-white curtain creates a diffused
light which is excellent for reducing the bright
contrasts.

13
Bedroom with bunks in a weekend home furnished by
architect P. Menichetti. Again, the whole effect is
based on vividly contrasting colours. The space is used
very economically.

14-15-17

Dressing room and bedroom for two teenagers. The furniture is reduced to essentials and colour is a fundamental element of the décor. A picture rail runs the length of the walls, making it easy to move the paintings about as desired. The girl's room (photo 15) is characterized by the white lacquered wood shelving.

14   15

16

The ideal division into bed area and study area, in this young girl's room, is brought about by means of the low shelving against which the bed rests. The armchair by the desk is by Knoll. The rounded bedside table was designed by Castiglioni for Kartell. The colour scheme of the walls and the dark carpet create a warm and relaxed atmosphere.

16

17

18
An original and sophisticated bedroom for a Paris flat.
Wooden ceiling, floor and walls in white polished
bricks, and brick is used again for some of the fittings
including the bed base. The leather settee is designed
by Tobia Scarpa for Gavina.

The attic

Attic – here it is possible to escape the limitations imposed by the usual square shape of modern flats: the sloping ceiling, odd angles and irregular shape are full of possibilities. It may be used as a study, a hobby room, or a children's playroom, and even, where space permits, a small flat.

1
Attic used as a study in a country house furnished by
Studio Tetrarch. White lacquered wooden beaded
ceiling, lacquered wood bookcase and wall, with glass
sections. A notable feature is the fireplace, with its tall
white plastered chimney, attached to the low walnut
units.

2
This cheerful room for children has been created in the
attic of a weekend home; note the thick roof beams.
The beds are placed in a raised section covered in
moquette. Big, bright posters decorate the sand-white
varnished walls. Furnished by OPS studio.

2

3–4
Attic living-room in a mountain dwelling, furnished by
architect G. Rebecchini. The materials and colours of
the fixtures and furniture are almost uniform, based on
the colours of the wood, the room's dominant feature.
The large stone fireplace dominates the rear wall.

3

4

5
The attic of this house in Germany has been adapted as
a combined living-room and study and furnished in
simple, austere lines. Le Corbusier chairs produced by
Cassina. Furnished by architects Witzemann and
Stadelmaier.

5

6
In an attic with a recess a tiny flatlet has been made
consisting of a multi-purpose room and a bedroom and
services. Furnished by Graziella Lonardi. The all-over
moquette flooring is by the same designer.

7
The attic of an old country house, turned into a study.
The old wooden beams have been painted in white
enamel, giving an effect of lightness which masks their
massive, rustic quality and transforms them into
elements of decoration.

Decoration

Decoration – this may be developed in one of two ways: the traditional method of using paintings, drawings, engravings and small sculptures, and the method seen in some of the examples shown here, which consists of drawing and painting straight on to the walls. Decorative schemes of the latter kind can make even the most ordinary room interesting and lively. Posters are particularly effective in a young person's room.

1
Detail of the living-room in Vasarely's home. The rigid
geometrical forms of the painting are typical of the
artist's work and dominate the room, as well as being
reflected in the low glass-topped table; the simple
geometrical shapes of the small fireplace and armchairs
are closely allied to the painting.

Two views of an art collector's living-room. Furnished by architect G. Veneziani. The room is made lively and attractive by the quality of the works of art decorating its walls and by the way they are arranged (without

3

regard to relationships and symmetries other than those dictated by the forms and colours of the works themselves) and by the objects furnishing the room.

4
Another example of an asymmetrical arrangement of paintings and drawings, which is carefully based on colour relationships, in an interior furnished by Natalia Aspesi.

4

5
The decorative feature chosen for the wall of this entrance to a dental surgery is a large red arrow pointing to the waiting rooms. This may be thought rather menacing in this particular setting, but it is undoubtedly effective and attractive. Furnished by Archinstudio.

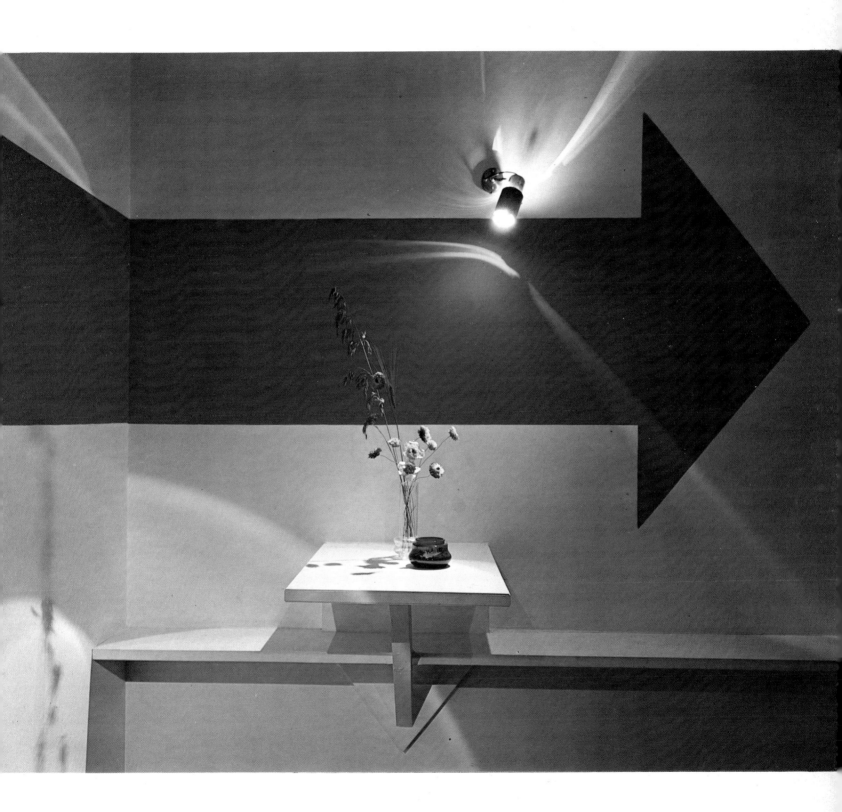

6

7

8

6-7-8
A house which is certainly most unusual, where the
decoration has been made an integral part of the
furnishing. It is the home of Richard Ohrbach, a young
American designer. Almost the only material used is
plastic, and with this Ohrbach has organized a
continuous space, structured mainly by means of light
and wall partitions. The traditional appearance of the
various rooms of a flat has been discarded in favour of
a single multi-purpose space in which fitted service
elements have been inserted. The use of a single
material throughout gives the whole area a unity which
could not otherwise be obtained.

9
In this dining corner, the brightly coloured decoration
is of primary importance and imparts its character to the
room. Designed by Adriano Campioni.

10–11–12
In this example, designed in New York by Norma Aronson and Tom Eubank, decoration is again the most important element in the whole décor. A rainbow-coloured strip leads from the entrance hall to the large living-room graphic. Almost the whole wall and ceiling

10

11

surfaces, as well as the sparse furniture, are white, a silent commentary on the feast of colours in the huge graphic. In the small photos we see the point at which the walls and ceiling meet. The shape of the room is modified by the decoration, which extends the space by its brilliant sequence of colours.

13–14
The Paris home of architect Yona Friedman. Drawings,
fabrics, books and small wooden objects all participate
in the decoration, furnished with independence and
assured taste.

15 *Overpage*
An example of how the corner of an everyday living-
room may be modified by a simple, effective wall
decoration. Simple bands of colour echo the bright
tones of the cushions. Designed by architect Nani
Prina.

16 *Overpage*
In this simple bedroom, furnished by architects
Gramigna and Mazza, a lively and attractive décor is
created at little cost by means of posters and large
photos freely arranged on the walls.

17 *Overpage*
In this living-room for a small flat in a mountain area
the designer has made skilful use of wall units to hold
bottles and crockery. He has used their formal values
to enrich the space, so that the objects are no longer
simply functional. Furnished by Piero Menichetti.

16

The bathroom

Bathroom – in the average flat there is little scope for substantial change in the bathroom; the fixed position of the door, window and apparatus limits the designer to a choice of coverings or possibly a new set of fittings. However, even within these limits, colour and good design are effective, as can be seen from the following examples.

1
Even in a bathroom one can hang original paintings. In
fact, in this décor by Isabelle Hebey the colour tone of
Poliakoff's painting becomes the focal point around
which the entire colour scheme of the room is
developed. Walls covered in canvas, floors in nylon
carpeting.

1

2

2
Another bathroom designed by Isabelle Hebey. The
inclusion of the small figure and bookshelves testify to
a desire to make a more habitable room out of one
which is usually considered strictly functional.

3

4

5

3
A bathroom completely covered in red laminated plastic. This material has changed an ordinary room into a new and unconventional one.

4
An elegant bathroom designed by Isabelle Hebey for a Paris flat. At the end of the bath is an indoor flower garden. The bath itself is covered in aluminium; the walls are lacquered white and the ceiling is glossy. Tobacco-coloured nylon moquette flooring.

5
Another stylish and tasteful bathroom furnished by Isabelle Hebey. Walls and storage units covered in laminated plastic. Nylon moquette flooring. Window blind with vertical slats which can be arranged as desired.

6 The walls of this modernized bathroom are covered in laminated plastic to conceal the old tiles. The long wooden shelf is an enormously useful addition. Beige carpeting.

7 The distinctive feature of this bathroom furnished by Martine Dufour is the use of white laminated plastic

6

throughout for all the furniture as well as the wall surfaces. The only colour in this austere setting is provided by the cushions, small plants and towels.

8 Traditional bathroom with deep blue tiles from the Cedit range for the floor and paler blue tiles for the walls.

7

8